Second Line Home

Second Line Home
New Orleans Poems

Mona Lisa Saloy

New Odyssey Series
Truman State University Press
Kirksville, MO

Cover art: *Bring it back; bring it all back (The Mothers of New Orleans)*, by Richard C.
Thomas, New Orleans, Louisiana.

Cover design: Teresa Wheeler

Library of Congress Cataloging-in-Publication Data
Saloy, Mona Lisa.
[Poems. Selections]
Second line home : New Orleans poems / by Mona Lisa Saloy.
pages cm
Includes bibliographical references.
ISBN 978-1-61248-100-5 (Paperback : alk. paper) — ISBN 978-1-61248-101-2 (E-book)
I. Title.
PS3619.A439A6 2014
811'.6—dc23
                                                                    2013045538

To The Most High God, source of all favors, so many blessings, and
strength to continue with joy.
To all Crescent City folks who returned to rebuild
one brick,
one board,
one wall at a time.
To friends far and wide, volunteers, well wishers, contributors,
families and friends, of us all, who prayed with us,
helped us, and listened while we persevered.
To our ancestors who paved our way with great gifts and sacrifices.
Red beans thanks!

Contents

See You in the Gumbo

First Line: Requiem for the Crescent City

La Vie Créole & Étoufée Talk

Hurricanes & Hallelujahs

Presidential Poems

Second Lines: New Orleans Matters

Acknowledgments

Completion of this manuscript was made possible by generous grants from the New Orleans Jazz & Heritage Festival Foundation, the UNCF/Mellon Foundation, and the Andrew Mellon Foundation in a year-long sabbatical leave from Dillard University.

"Missing in 2005: New Orleans Neighborhood Necessities" appears in *The Southern Poetry Anthology*, Vol. 4, *Louisiana*, edited by Paul Ruffin and William Wright (Texas Review Press, 2010).

"On Not Being Able to Write a Poem, to New Orleans Post Katrina" (here in a slightly different form) and "For the New Young Bloods on My Porch" were first published in *Pan African Literary Journal* 4, no. 2 (Fall 2010).

"Les Pains Des Creoles" premiered on Susan Larson's *The Reading Life*, WWNO Public Radio, November 22, 2011.

"We" was first published in *Konch,* 2006.

"Blessed Be U" appears in an earlier form in the *God Stories* issue of *Louisiana Literature* (16/1, 1999).

See You in the Gumbo

See You in the Gumbo

Soon as humidity rears its head in mid-May,
We smell the rainy season coming.
Gotta get out the grill, stoke some coals,
Braise some shrimp; soak some red beans
Steam that rice, and enjoy galleries,
Yards, and back porches,
Party with a DJ spinning Johnny Adams' "Tell It Like It Is."
      Dance like nobody's there
      Dance like nobody's there

Spring spreads aphids on roses
Something about the morning mist a
Kiss to every blade of grass and iris bud
Graduations grow like mushrooms in spring, by
Memorial Day, backyard barbeques
Rise like the sun beaming everywhere
Folks don't make no never mind about June first
Hurricane hype from TV weather watchers. Just count flashlights,
Candles in jars, canned tuna, peanut butter, water,
Water, bottled, jugged, stacked in cases
Party with family crooners
      Dance like nobody's there
      Dance like nobody's there

Atlantic & Gulf waters stir first swirls
Daily news broadcasts brace for
Tropical storms turning into hurricanes
Hurry now, stock up on supplies
Storm warnings rise like cream in café au lait
Folks don't make no never mind about
Hurricane season starts, we

Joke about Hurricane Betsy whose waters flowed
Down streets like a parade with
Floating bodies of dogs, cats, people, shrimp, swollen stinky, we
Party, shake off the coat of fear with a DJ spinning Joe Jones'
       "You talk too much, you worry me to death . . ."
    Dance like nobody's there; dance like nobody's there,
Gas up the car, pack emergency lights, shout
See you in the gumbo! See you in the gumbo!
    Dance like nobody's there! See you in the gumbo!

Sankofa NOLA

Our names return three or
Four centuries to ancestors
Shipped here like sardines,
Saltwater Africans coupled to
Euro English, Irish, French, German, Italian, Spanish,
Portuguese, or Natives Choctaw, Houma,
Natchez, and Alabama, others far & wide. These
Families with roots like the
Live oaks firmly planted then arms
Embracing & arching over like an umbrella
Against torrential wars, winds,
Diseases, disappointments
Bring our African selves & souls to
Echo from Cuba, Haiti, and all points Caribbean, Central American, to
Carve lives into New Orleans, Caribbean North, into neighborhoods
    like Gentilly,
Sugar Hill, Tremé, Pallet Land, so many others
Resonating into celebrating births, baptisms,
Confirming cultural dances of sorrow songs,
Blues, jazz, reggae, and burying our dead in rocking
Home-going gospel celebrations with horse-drawn
Carriages of solemn dirges of grief then
Handkerchief flying trombone blasting
Second Line dances celebrating a life well lived, so
We can cry, smile, and continue masking until the next Mardi Gras.
There's a whole lot of praying in between, the altar
Candles lit in promises of faith, the novenas of
Devotion to our Lord, venerating saints like Anne, Joseph & saving
    sinners,
Cleansing souls, and blessing each day, each week, each decade, each
Century, the promise of better for generations to come.

Not hurricanes, not tornadoes, not torrential shifts can
Sway such steady faith and love of God, family, community
Firmly planted for centuries, Creoles
Who know how to live well and do daily: *la joie de vivre* ain't no big
    mati
Love always, committed to caring
One family, one block, one church, many Cubans, Haitians, Puerto
    Rican Creole
Cultures together celebrating each one's crafts
Teaching each one's generations grounded in this
Crescent City landscape of camellia, bougainvillea, hydrangea, iris in
'Sippi & Ponchartrain clay, with swamp, 'squitoes & sunshine.

Evacuation Blues
This is how we did it

TV weather news paints Gulf-sized hurricane swirls. I
Clear debris from the backyard, pack lawn chairs
Tie yard tools in the shed; a phone blasts eternal:

> "Are you leaving?' Miz Ruth squeaks between TV blasts of
> doom.
> "No indeed. We'll be alright like always."

Ruth Zeno Barnes knew me before I was born. Her
Dad, master carpenter, built the first home on our block, her
Brother a Silver Star Purple Heart Hero Infantryman in WWII.
Her parents, friends to my grandparents, she & hubby
Friend to my mom, dad—his late wife, Dee, my aunts, uncles, siblings.
When Dee drank her last bourbon & Coke for breakfast,
Ruth made red beans in Dee's big pot, later Miz Ruth
Kept it too as a memory of her friend then
Fed my dear doggie, Jasmine, when I traveled for research.

Phone rings won't stop, eerie sputtering, ringing on and on
Cousin Dwight on the line, tells of Con Con, his wife's
Dreams of water everywhere, and turn on the TV. This
Is the big one. Doppler radar paints Katrina swirls spanning the
Entire Gulf of Mexico headed dead for us, New Orleans.

> "D, you staying like we usually do right?" I

Depend on my dear cousin, my brother, his front
Yard walking distance, just a couple of blocks, screaming close.

Miz Ruth packs quickly fussing about how I just said we're
Staying, and will be fine, but Dwight's telling of

Con Con's dream. She & Dwight, mother, father
Singing musicians, music ministers of faith, from St. Raymond to
      Xavier U.,
Both born to crooning dads of music, and moms of beauty and
      strength.
Con Con, *bona fide* blessed to see; her dreams come true.
Connie rides night fire for visions, avalanches of answers in dreams.
Con Con a force of good and gladness with each smile, each
Shrimp or crab dinner cooked and shared with love and answers from
      dreams.

Couldn't believe my ears. Now what? A frantic 360 view of books,
      movies,
Music on CDs, classic 33 rpm's. Take what? Elder neighbor Ruth
      Barnes cries
        "You said we're staying," from her backyard.
I pack PJs, student comp. papers to grade, a change of clothes, nothing
      too fancy,
Comfort for the drive, a few gallons of water, fruit, nuts, dog food,
      extra doggie treats,
Jasmine riding in rear of my red 4Runner, happy for a wide window &
      bacon bits aroma steaming. I call Dwight & Con Con again,
        "Water was everywhere; I can't explain it."
        "Dwight, you sure?"
        "Sweetie, we've all gotta go!"

We went, by auto by truck by wagon by SUV
By diesel with families, friends, neighbors
Waving hands to families, friends, neighbors
Across contraflow interstate lanes, all going to
All points out of here.

Miz Ruth and I each had one small bag, a rain jacket, and
We adjusted auto arrangements until cozy. A widow now,
Miz Ruth buried her son, Michael, a few years past; he was my

Knee baby. At five, he held my hand for the half-dozen blocks to
Epiphany Catholic School, a beautiful boy, a little brother more than a
Neighbor, whose illness was heavy on all our hearts. Miz Ruth, still
    there for
Me, Jasmine, Miz Velma, Mr. Lou, family, all the elders on my block,
    blessed
We left as Mayor Nagin calls for the first citywide evacuation in
    history, Sunday, midday.

We were bumper to bumper for hours, the
Sun high over our heads, we waving at cousins in caravan, other
Church folks in contraflow lanes, all traffic fanned akimbo from the
Crescent City praying for safe passage, affirming that
"Nothing can happen that God can't handle." Then, we sing along
    with
94.5 FM, the Praise Station blasts Fred Hammond:
        "We shall mount up on wings
        Like an eagle and soar . . .
        They that wait on the Lord, wait on the Lord . . ."
Rows of traffic, cars, trucks, in lanes like ants to anywhere safe,
Stopping in lines unable to move 45 minutes at a time, then
Longer. Jasmine happy looking out of the picture window, then
Nightfall outside of Baton Rouge eight hours later, Miz Ruth & I
    dancing in our seats, I
Call Cindy La
        "Just need to visit the little girls' room, walk Jassie . . .
        We can sleep in this truck, don't want to put y'all out."
        "No, don't worry."
        "It's not just me, Cindy, I have Miz Ruth and Jasmine too."
        "Just come," Cindy says, and we did, camped out in her
Living room, me on the floor, Miz Ruth on a couch, Jasmine between
    us.

First Line
Requiem for the Crescent City

August Landing & Katrina Hits

An endless night of newscasts of fear and wind beating windows,
   doors about to burst,
Roofs knocking loudly, surely monsters make less noise.

TV news reports car crashes while evacuating, images of NOLA
   emptying of folks like
Sacks of marbles running or like water spread in every direction.

Winds wail through wee hours; bigger branches beat windows,
   rooftops, and bomb doors like a war zone rattling shrapnel, then
   lights fail; the television blackens.

Cindy's hubby, Terry, legally blind biologist, sweet tempered, sharp wit
   sees
Women worrying wishing for "we talk," escapes with Bella, their dog, to
Save Jasmine's fear. Jassie finds other dogs uncouth, probably about
   them humping
More than play. Bella tiptoes around Jassie. Terry brokers peace
   between them.

No one sleeps. Storm surges sound sprays, breaks windows nearby,
Windows pained by pressure.
We pray in Creole, English, and Hebrew. *Papa nou.* Our Father.
   Hallelujah.
Too scared to talk anymore, silence sends sleep.

Daylight wakes us early. We give thanks for daylight calm.
Doors swollen with water open to debris as
Far as the eye can see
More trees in streets than on land
Live oak broken branches spread

Across Cindy & Terry's lawn
Like salad spread.
Roads not passable
Cable lines down
No lights yet
No TV. No news
No phone signals
Cell phone texts escape the silence
Cindy's artist dad & retired bookseller mom on their way for shelter.
Terry & I pile tree limbs in mounds near the street.
Hours later, grass appears; triumphant, Terry rakes again.
Miz Ruth and I pack night clothes before moving on to somewhere
Thankful for Cindy & Terry's open hearts and home.

On not being able to write a post-Katrina poem about New Orleans

It wasn't Katrina you see
It was the levees
One levee crumbled under Ponchartrain water surges
One levee broke by barge, the one not supposed to park near Ninth-
    Ward streets
One levee overflowed under Ponchartrain water pressure
We paid for a 17-foot levee but
We got 10-foot levees, so
Who got all that money—the hundreds of thousands
Earmarked for the people's protection?

No metaphors capture this battle for New Orleans
Now defeated and scorned by the bitter mistress of Bush-era
    non-government
New Orleans is broken by the bullet of ignorance
Our streets are baptized by brutal neglect
Our homes, now empty of brown and white faces, segregated by
Our broken promises of help where only hurt remains
Our hearts like our voices hollow now in the aftermath

Our eyes are scattered among TV images of
Our poor who without cars cling to interstate ramps like buoys
Our young mothers starving stealing diapers and bottles of baby food
Our families spread as ashes to the wind after cremation
Our brothers our sisters our aunts our uncles our mothers our fathers
    lost
Stranded like slaves in the Middle Passages
Pressed like sardines, in the Superdome, like in slave ships

Where there was no escape from feces or
Some died on sidewalks waiting for help
Some raped in the Dome waiting for water and food
Some kids kidnapped like candy bars on unwatched shelves
Some beaten by shock and anger
Some homeless made helpless and hopeless by it all

Where is Benjamin Franklin when we need him?
Did we not work hard, pay our taxes, vote our leaders into office?
What happened to life, liberty, and the pursuit of the good?
Oh say, can you see us America?
Is our bright burning disappointment visible six months later?
Is all we get the baked-on sludge of putrid water, your empty
    promises?
Where are you America?

Missing in 2005
New Orleans Neighborhood Necessities

Mothers and fathers order the day
Girls may clean clothes; boys scour steps
Aunts bake and send bread pudding out for tasty replies
Grandmothers guard knee babies
Grandfathers eye the progress of dovetail joints or the
Pouring of new pavement
Uncles spin their latest fast steps or two-for-a-nickle tales
Here, history and culture paint our days in an endless fan stroke.
Schooled or street taught, the past sticks to us like sugar on beignets

Mondays, mothers slow-cook red beans and rice
Fathers bring home hands hardened by
Knuckle-breaking work and handshakes
Grandmothers and grandfathers join weekend suppers and
Front-porch rendezvous
Graceful sorrow songs lace the day, or early-morning Nat King Cole
    moves to
Afternoon rhythm and blues meters' style,
Heartfelt hints of love overcoming hurt
Evening praise music is hip enough to hear daily
Night-time Ibraham melodies echo lifetimes of urban haunts,
Bullet's Bar, The Parakeet, Winnie's Place, hanging on corners
Boys carry trumpets or tubas and belt tunes on the walk home
Girls or guys sing retooled EWF: Earth, Wind & Fire, remix they call it,
While waiting for the St. Bernard Avenue bus
St. Augustine's Marching 100 practices in Hardin Park after school
Serenading the neighborhood with big band versions of Earth, Wind &
    Fire's "Never"

Corpus Christi, Epiphany, or St. Raymond Church choirs belt Sunday
    ballads
Peopled by parishioners who practice throughout the week
Neighborhood kids grow into choir directors and piano players or
Soloists on Sundays or Saturday vigil masses
Some sing at Baptist churches, Beecher Memorial, or Fifth African
    Baptist,
Mount Zion, African-Methodist-Episcopalian, others where
Saturday nights see them singing and making music in nightclubs
    across town
Social Aid and Pleasure Clubs parade and hire bands to
Pour music into every street; sidewalk audiences blossom and bloom
    while
Dancing behind step parades or Second Line bands.
Such training ground is free flowing, like the humid air,
Heavy with humidity, heart, sweat, and elbow grease

September 2005, New Orleans

They said only businesses could come into the city,
First, then residents by zip code. New Orleans is all
Our business, so I went by rent-a-car with the
Good husband—Rich—of my dear colleague at DU.
No traffic from Baton Rouge for many miles,
Riding along swamp and southern evergreens
Still standing, like tall pines, a few magnolias.

Traffic slowed stacked, like toys, past Causeway
At the 610 Interstate split. Armed GIs in fatigues say:
"State your business."

Once in the neighborhood, the smell of death
Laced streets, covered in debris along the sidewalks,
Enough room to pass, with some live wires popping,
No sign of anything alive, no birds chirping, no
'squitoes buzzing, no cats crossing, no dogs running,
No people here, downtown, no cars either, just empty
Silence, so loud, like the dead ghost towns of the old West.

Before our government heard, before churches came, before
Volunteers showed up to help, the only
Beacon of light downtown, shining
Like the Christmas star: Bullet's Bar on
A.P. Tureaud with ice for the weary, food and drinks for
Neighborhood men drudging debris,
Digging their homes out from the muck
Camping in their trucks
Parked high on the neutral grounds like at Mardi Gras time.

When I saw bodies

When I see bodies bent to fold on cars
When I smell death across the lines of fence
Bodies rot soft so left to stink on bars
Whole families broken no recompense
A car's antenna so straight and stuck
On men on boys to fit a shirt so stretched
To keep bodies I see in place just lost
You see their trunks so arched as made to freeze
I would prefer to wake or have them smile
A frame for families such loss to grieve
No one stands straight but limp to snatch a dream
Upward to God for true just grief to scream

New Orleans
Broken Not Dead

—*kudos to Claude McKay*

If we must break and lose our land to them
Hunted and penned in an inglorious dome,
From signs and lies and tales too tall to find
Making their mock at our drowned homes
While round us each to sweep to dig to build
With wood with brick with steel so strong and clean
Our culture food our dance we love to live
Though first outnumbered, we ache we show us brave
Our craftsmen carve and pour our iron our wood
In vain for months we search our loves our lost
Then build one wall one floor one door one roof
The stench the dead so long in heat with us
Like men and women, bold, we make our pact,
Pressed to our knees, held down but kicking back!

Post-Katrina
Summer, 2007

Today it's 88 degrees outside.
Inside the Tulane hospital emergency
Waiting room, the AC a
Quiet comfort like
Sister Claudia Marie
Under headdress & habit of
Black & white, a
Holy Family nun.
We swap stories of aging
Bodies, she with nerve-damaged
Feet and heart attacks
After Katrina, a bulging
Knuckle that tells the weather.
I tell of my hit & run, a
Small white compact at
7:30 in the morning before
Sunday service, being bumped
Up onto the hood, sliding sideways &
Snagged by the side-view mirror, the
White compact swerving forward
Gravity sliding me stuck, the
Pulling, shoulder pain, then
Slipping toward the sidewalk,
Fred, a runner coming to my aid,
My cousin Connie in shock that
She escaped the compact's smack, me
Her bumper.
My hand to God:
Didn't break a bone.
Sister Claudia smiles

Like a happy Buddha.
I tell of missing daily walks
Early morning meditations of
Thanks, the overgrown oaks &
Frayed evergreens half wild.
"Sister Claudia, will you recover soon?"
"If God says the same."
We swap smiles & amens.

New Orleans in January

White camellias stretch and flap wide like gardenias
Pink, red, yellow roses bloom fat with petals arched like open umbrellas
Trees and shrubs defy the control of
Brick, mortar, or iron bars like the
Wild roses that
Trellis along wrought-iron and wooden fences.
King cakes compete for rare dollars, their
Politically correct plastic babies no longer just pink/red white, now
     boast
Chocolate, gold, silver, even yellow, green bodies inside,
Emblem of food fortune for the year, like the three kings
Seeking the baby Jesus, once found, blessed for another year.
Wild ducks and geese laugh and tease motorists
Along Bayou St. John, Moss Street, passing Esplanade Avenue,
Not a care in the grasses, some more brown than green.
Angel trumpets and night jasmine fragrance dusk
When the moon rises in eastern skies smiling.

Poems like Cell Phones

One day while waiting for Chris in Engineering
Some words flew into my head.
Such intrusions vex the soul
Like when I'm downloading software updates and the
CPU won't cooperate, some ad for face cream or
15 chances to win $10,000.
"Yeah, ya' right!" Or, while
Checking on the southerly breezes from the Gulf or surfing
Gulf water temperatures to gage the safety of eating oysters, musing
Is it an *R* month? Then
Poems break into thought like a noisy mosquito biting a forearm
Whizzing incessantly, insisting on being heard and felt, or when a
Cell phone buzzes or rings
Who is it? Will they call again? Or will the
Message fly forever?

For the New Young Bloods on My Porch

Two years two months after post-Katrina flooding, I remember the
First time I saw y'all
      Camped out, sitting on my front porch
      Chilled out in the cool shade of my cement stoop
      Spread-eagle on the steps like you owned the place
      Bronzed chocolate faces, all sizes, ages, and you
      Acted like you owned the place,
I welcomed you,
Told you, seeing y'all reminded me of my brother and his friends
      standing guard for our block, our street, our neighborhood
      though sometimes they stole a smoke from big butts on the
      street
      or made fun of people passing by
      or they played coon can in the street, stopping traffic
There y'all are, the new neighborhood residents
Bringing life to this Seventh Ward New Orleans block struggling to
    return to glory.
Come to think of it, I
      should have taken names
      should have found y'all mommas & dads
      should have checked if you were in school, and where
      should have checked to see whether you could read and write
      should have thrown 20 questions to test for any common sense
      should have jacked you up for being so cocky
            when y'all ran my tap till the bill burned me
            lining up cars to wash on my dime
            leaving the water running for its source,
            y'all not caring for the holes you make in my pockets.

Then, in the last two weeks,
I wouldn't be so shocked to find my 100-year-old cypress doors &
    windows destroyed,
My cement and bricks—formed by Creole craftsmen—broken like
    rotten teeth, and
Y'all grinnin' like Stepin Fetchit, slitherin' away.

Grief and Loss

Afraid, tired Black faces
Men and women
Boys and girls—
Fanned akimbo on the Superdome stairs
Brown faces flash on TV sets of
Temperature-controlled homes
These stranded families, neighbors,
Strangers once, now forced into
Photo-op status for front-page horror
These Black faces—
Loss and grief
Like thorns in America's flag
Their points dulled
By a democratic ideal out of reach
Grief and loss
Black faces
Still at war with American justice,
Just us
Still thirsty for peace
And a home.

Grief

Sneaks up on you
Like an elegant
Pussy cat coasting
Along with steps barely
Touching anything solid,
Floating in waves,
Then quicker than spit
Grief scratches your skin
Till it bleeds all the bottled-
Up hurt, past knocks, and
Future breaths.

Iraq by the Numbers

Five years ago, 2007, the
U.S. of A.
Bombed Baghdad
Flattened world history with
Ancient artifacts
Exposed in the rubble.
Then, someone stole the
Code of Hammarabi Code, the
Oldest record of human writing.
Hundreds of bombs lighting the night sky
Like comets impaling earth.
4,000 Americans killed,
24,000 U.S. soldiers killed
Many broken for life
2,000,000 Iraqis move out of
Their country,
Hundreds of thousands of Iraqis
Crushed into crumbs,
Their neighborhoods smashed,
Artifacts of humanity looted
Like the lives of young and old.
The sea is painted with their blood.

My Race

Ah, my race
My throbbing race
Bronze beauties burnt
By disappointments
Since God knows when.
Still from pyramids
To spirituals,
To rhythm & blues,
Soul, soul food,
Creole food,
Cajun food,
The blues,
Jazz,
Reggae,
Still laughing to keep sane.
Despite lynchings,
Racism, prejudice,
Walking while Black,
Glass ceilings,
Brick walls,
Emmett Till,
41 bullets shot at Diallo in NYC,
The Texas dismemberment by car,
Deflated dreams of equality, and
The fact that African Americans still
Scrape for crumbs of the American pie,
Turns out,
There's no such thing as race.
So why is skin color still the
People's plague?

2 Friends

—for Cindy Lou Levee

We met in San Francisco
She was Levy from Uptown New Orleans
Me, Saloy from the Seventh Ward, downtown
She a Jew and middle class
Me a Catholic, Creole, working class
We both love Anne Frank, Du Bois, Lillian Hellman & Zora Neale
    Hurston
We've been friends through dozens of performances and walks
2 states
4 cities
5 faiths between us (add Buddhism, Baha'i, Religious Science)
Always searching for God, we have
1 shared spiritual homeland, Israel
4 cavaliers (gentlemen friends)
1 husband 1 son
4 parents, 2 gone to glory now
7 siblings, 2 gone to glory
6 universities, 2 grad schools, 4 graduate degrees between us
3 organizations, from Southern Women to the DeBose Fine Arts
3 arts councils; 4 dogs: Dufas, Bella, Jass, Julie
2 cats: Tuscan, April, all gone to old age or illness
6 hurricanes, 2 earthquakes: 1 in San Francisco, 1 on the Oakland/
    Berkeley border
3 plays, 10 manuscripts
35 plus winters &
Many more springs.

Meanwhile, back in America

New Orleans still lies broken.
Had to take cold showers in November 2006
While water remains in the gas lines,
Yet the bill is times four HIGHER than before the unnatural flooding.
Miz Juanita's got no phone service yet,
Her house gutted, reeking of mold, boarded, frowning
Frame and cypress doors hint of past glory and gladness.
Housing rentals rise four times too. By next April, the
Grass returns, but how can the folks?

La Vie Créole & Étoufée Talk

Les Pains des Creoles / Creole Breads

Pour les Creoles / For Creoles
No dinner
No lunch
No snack
No meal is complete without
Our bread! *Pour diné*
Le pain de la Français
French bread.
Hey *la bas mais oui*!

Oh les Creoles
We are Love, *nous sommes amour*
Nous pains, our breads,
Le pain de perdue / Lost bread or
Gallait, pan-fried flat bread
Dipped in pure cane syrup, maybe honey
Pour la petite dejeuner / for breakfast
Le pain de la Français / French bread
For dipping in vinaigrette
Pure and virgin oils anointing tongues
Cheeks, lips, lingering
At sundown *avec /* with salad
Or just lemon, garlic, and butter for spread
With *panné* meat (breaded veal cutlets) or
Cawain, turtle, in season or
Just enough to sop Crawfish Monica.

Les pains des Creoles
Creole breads,
Make the body of a meal
One

Z'Haricots Rouge   Red Beans

Z'erbs (Z'Hericots) rouge	red beans
Amis rouge	red friends
Amis amour	friend love
Noir amour	black love
Amour rouge	red love
Couyon amour	idiot love
Goûte amer	tastes bitter
Avec amour	with love
Amour	love
Goûte bonne	tastes good
Goûte comme plus	tastes like more

For Uncle Herbert

Way back in the days
They called
My chocolate Creole-
Crooning upright-piano-playing
Uncle Herbert
Shunk, no *grand mati*
Stuck to him like
Skunk spray; couldn't
Wash it or wish it off, a name
Worn on thick, its origin
Faded with years,
He called me "Niecey"
Like I was a little Buddha or royalty
Soon as I entered a room he sang
My theme song, "Mona Lisa"
At five I knew he wrote it just for me, then
I learned it was everybody's song, only
Uncle Herbert sang it special to me.

In the neighborhood
Reggie Dixon, who blew sax for the
Crescent City Sound Company, a
Big R&B band, 9 pieces, 3 horns,
Playing the Vieux Carré weekly in those days,
Reggie's mom,
Gloria, called Uncle Herbert
Warm; that was his way, his sound
Tickling black & white ivory keys
88 love notes with his silky voice
Warm

For Herbert Jr.

—a.k.a Frances

Herbert Jr. ran from the
Crescent City at 16.
Schools couldn't hold him, so
Good-looking folks wanted to
Call him "Sugar," but him being a
Manchild, they settled for
"Shagoo."

In Los Angeles, he was
Frances, an actor in
Dinner theatres, made it to
The Bold & The Beautiful.
Man, proud can't contain
Our joy. Then he came
Home, back on the block; and
Even with his eyes sad
Heavy with personal hurricanes
He passed away, leaving only
Dapper memories, his
Grace on the dance floor, from
Salsa to the cha-cha, with
Shakespeare on his lips,
Carved ivory queens from
Cameroon on our library shelves,
Us in his heart
Herbert in ours, Shagoo, but we call him
Frances like he asked.

Katrina Daze

Some 72 months past post-Katrina flooding
past the first cold winter I remember since
snow laced rooftops in New Orleans in 2004.
Northerners ask, how do you manage in that humid air?
We Black Creoles do as Jelly Roll Morton sings:

"thought he heard Buddy Bolden shout.
Open up that window, and let that bad air out!
Open up that window, and let the foul air out!
Yeah. Like Buddy Bolden says!
 Open up that window, and let that bad air out!"

Front porches or galleries are good for that,
Airing out stale talk and leftover dinners and
Bad news like the umteenth change in Road-to-Home rules.
We must elevate, says the three-foot rule,
Whether you're more than that below sea level.

Another neighbor's gone to glory.
At 84, Mr. Lou, classmate of "Tootie" Montana—great Big Chief of the
     Yellow Pocahontas,
Those Black men who mask yearly making Carnival for us in
     neighborhoods
When Negroes were not allowed uptown on Mardi Gras Day.
The press calls them Mardi Gras Indians; we call them Black Indians.
That's what they are,
Warriors waging culture to cure jim crow rules and
Lively up our streets in bursts of ostrich feathers and
Beads telling our stories.

My Creole neighbor, Mr. Lou, drove 18-wheelers
For Domino Sugar, turning his big rig 'round the street like a toy.
Like his smile, he brought us liquid sugar for flapjacks.
Mr. Lou came to civil court with me at least
Eight times, to rid my daddy's house
Of crackheads, who just moved in
When Daddy forgot who he knew.
My neighbor stood up for me, he said, like my dad would if he could.
After that, he fed my dog Jassie treats, watched the house and me until
    home safely.
His home-going is Friday.

December 2005
at Stephanie's House

—*For the Lipps family*

One of the only homes for blocks
That didn't flood.
       She had a guardian angel!
       God saved their home!

Stephie's guilt weighs like
Soaked mounds of sofas, settees, wardrobes. . . .
My cousin, my brother,
My cousin, my sister ask
       Why me?
       Why not?
We know, those huddled here like
Fingers, water-soaked and wrinkled:
       God knew we needed a spot to hang
       Caring for our flooded-out homes.
       Thank God for Stephie and Warren.

We half sit, half stand
In Stephanie & Warren's kitchen,
Our lives then, what we knew like backyard Sunday brunches,
Our eyes stare, our minds blank.
We hug tight, we rejoice
We again, after months gone
Our once-beautiful homes, memories now:
Connie's dad—Mush's Halloween b-day bashes
With gumbo, bus-stop line dances
Old-school swinging to Smokey Robinson
Fundraisers for St. Raymond Church

Or a bridal shower for a daughter, a cousin
The lovely yard soaked now in the stench of death,
One family at a time, returning
To find out what's left.

The Day Alzheimer's Showed

Daddy, what's wrong?
His Creole cheeks burnt rouge,
          "Victor, he's leaving the family. . ."
Daddy, who's Victor?
Is it the vegetable man
Who brings you jokes and
Brown paper bags of potatoes and
Corn from his neighborhood garden?
          "Ashley broke his heart. . ."
Ashley? Terry's baby girl?
Come on Daddy, how's that possible, and
Who is Victor?
His hazel eyes are steely blue
Like the Scottish plaid flannel shirt
He wears, his Marlboro hard pack
Standing at attention in his upper
Breast pocket on the left, an easy
Reach between coughs and near beer of
O'Douls in the can, cold as Canada or the
French Alps after snowfall.
At the door, a strawberry appears;
Her wig backwards, half dressed,
Bleeding from her lip like she kissed
More than two fists. Daddy jumps up,
Answers with me over his shoulder;
She tries to push her way inside.
I shut both doors. Who was that daddy?
          "*Pas connais*?" He shrugs, floating in and out of Creole
          "Ashley, . . . should have a cold one with me, . . .
          That woman ain't his wife no how."
A TV commercial boasts the softness of

Ivory detergent, towels floating like clouds in the heavens.
Music blares the Bill Bell theme song.
Two feet from my Dad's easy chair, his eyes
Drift; he sits up straight; his mid-80s body heavy, with Marlboro
    smoke,
Turns his head, looks at me sternly, the way Victor just did on
The Young and the Restless.

Alzheimer's, Day Two

"*Bébé*, get the door.
            Can't you hear that damned doorbell ringing?"
This Creole crazy man
Is my daddy, the
First man I loved,
At whose feet I read the funnies, the dictionary,
At whose side we read all the jokes in
The Reader's Digest,
At whose table we searched the
American Peoples Encyclopedia
To learn where Cuba sat and
Bahia rested on the Pacific and
Which was the biggest continent and
Where Panama split for its canal, the man-made
Gateway from one ocean to the other side.
            "Don't let no salespeople in here girl.
            Bébé? What's wrong with you?"
Daddy, it's Aunt Florence. He stares blankly.
Mother's little sister, you know, the
One you always say is peanut-butter-tan, cute, and
Drinks hot Jax beer from a long neck with Mother's smile and
Her pappa's forehead. Aunt Florence, Daddy,
Uncle Hookey's wife.
            "Hookey? Hookey who?"
Uncle Hookey, your brother-in-law,
Who always beat you at the horses?
Come and see, she's passing by
In the neighborhood, and . . .
He rocks up from his blue easy chair, a
Rare event unless for a bathroom run, and
Even I get his beers or ice cream. Water?

Who needs water when you can have a cold beer?

"*Bébé*, when water wasn't clean, people drank beer!"
Daddy. See, it's Aunt Florence, *Petite Flo*, you call her,
Shake your head as she guzzles hot Jax Beer.
His eyes are gunmetal grey today, and
Stare with questions bouncing eye to eye.

"I **don't** know **who** that is. Shut the door."

She was not a queen, but . . .

My mother's smooth skin,
Burnt chocolate brown, was
Bronzed by African ancestral birth,
Pink skin
Under her feet, hands, gums,
Grew past 58 years with
No wrinkles.
Midnights on each cheek,
Dawn rising in her smile;
In her eyes,
Silent Sheba queens blinking
Behind the panther in
Her steps.
Here she is ageless in the
Sepia photo circa 1943
Years, she wore a checkered blouse with a
Large white collar, a
Treasured gift from my big brother John,
Before she gave me a thought
Before she dropped me
On the back porch steps.
I wipe the mold carefully,
Caress her eyes with mine
Thankful her photo survives.

Missing Mother

My neck curves like mother said it would
If I didn't sit up. "Stand up straight or
You'll bend over like a person older than you are
When you're my age." When Mother's eyes saw me stoop,
My back straightened like a narrow balloon
Blown ready to make a stick figure for a clown.
Mother's eyes had a way of following me
Like a shadow, always there, just beyond sight,
Electric, like she had superpowers to make me
Smile at her wink; she liked to wink at me, and I
Melted each time, warmed over with
Her narrow brown eyes, the color of raw almonds.
Somewhere in the two weeks past 16, she left me,
Shriveled up like a blue prune, and
Left this life without saying goodbye. There
Was no one at the corner of my eyes
Slim and sparrow like hers, gone.
Why is God so full of love yet cruel?
Where are my mother's eyes?
Do her winks lace heaven?
For years, I carried her sayings on
My back like an alligator snapping
Stinging or hugging me for dear life. Now,
Her ways and wisdom are tucked
Neatly in a pocket, in my head
Sometimes, I forget her chocolate face
Smiling at me until I touch that space in
My pocket, the rough alligator skin familiar,
Its arms smaller over time, but its growl and
Bite, claws holds me again like today,
Dusting her framed face

Speaking to her sepia photo, damply dinged in
Katrina mold and humidity. It's hard to believe
I'm older than her last day,
She, a married mother as a teen, divorced soon after 20, then
Married again to my Creole Dad Louie, the second love of her life.
The first time Daddy saw Mother's beautiful teeth smiling at him,
He was in love, gave her the first taste of chocolate, the
Color of her cheeks like a frame. He taught her how to say *Bébé*—
Like my big brother John calls to me still today—and
Stew *cawain* in spring. Years later, at the
Dentist, Daddy cried at Mother's first painful cavity,
Her white white teeth flashing neon against ebony skin.
Near his last days, the guilt fell still from salty eyes.
Me, the baby girl grown now, and
Too long in the bad habit of slouching over stacks of books,
Book bags, magazines, microfilm, archives, journals old and new, me
Pregnant with papers to read and write, ideas stinging my head like
    'squitoes.
Today, from now on, I'm sitting and standing erect
Thankful for the dream of days and
Mother's wisdom packed in my pocket.

Creole Daddy Ways

My Creole daddy's first wife was
Caramel cute, 5 feet petite, had
Wavy hair like white folks, a
Cradle Catholic, church going regularly like
Waking up to sunshine. She was his
Sweetheart, warming the home front
When his long River Road trips
Kept him away nights
Delivering newly rolled tobacco
Packed like sardines in wooden boxes.
Then, something about one homecoming,
She asleep in the sheets she pressed so perfectly. Daddy said she
Broke his heart in half like a walnut split down the middle.

My Creole daddy's second wife was my mother,
Deep, dark chocolate, tall like me, 5'8", heavy boned, a
Black beauty he said often. She a PK,
Preacher's Kid, the eldest, the rock of her family,
Born and raised Baptist, Mount Zion style, had
No idea why my Creole daddy saw beauty in her face.
She could sew, grow roses like her *tchopitoulas* Mom,
Heal most cuts and ailments with herbs from the yard. From Baptist,
    Mother
Converted to Catholic to marry my Creole daddy, and that
Was the last time most saw him at church until his end.
My chocolate Creole mother was more Catholic than
My Creole daddy, he said, and she prayed enough for him. She
Prayed to the Blessed Mother and "practiced" healing
When folks needed it, few spells, only blessings. When
She passed, my world crushed like smashed pecans,
Scattered hope here, broken dreams there. I see

Her nose daily in my mirror; I kiss with her lips,
Smile with her eyes. She taught me to crochet when it rained for days, to
Find the beauty in any space of a home; and though
She feared water, I swam for her, brought home medals to
Assure her the kindness of water, and that
Negroes can swim. Okay, Okay, you swim for me she said.

My Creole daddy's last wife, DD, was tall &
Milk chocolate, rocking Baptist, and the
Rock of her family, raising nine kids alone,
Caring for her ailing father, a good Christian woman.
Like my mother, she sang any day. Mother sang Charles Brown's
    "Bells will be ringing. . ."
Any season, any time she had a mind to belt it out like a sneeze;
DD sang "Amazing Grace," all hours of the day staggering or sober.
DD was common and had little common sense, stayed drunk daily.
No big *MATI!*
Told me I was smart cause I earned my way, so I said
My Creole daddy insisted that I stand up for myself or
Have to lay down for anything or anyone,
Skills he said, a woman had to have some skills her own,
Just not too many, so she don't need a Colored man. DD's last
Daughter, about to graduate Joseph S. Clark High School like me, was
Killed going to the senior prom,
By a hit & run on the new Claiborne Avenue Interstate
Like me, she wanted college,
Choices a woman can make for herself.
She died instantly, and
Killed so much in DD, my Creole daddy's third wife.
Some say she drank herself to death, some say
DD had bourbon with a Coke back for breakfast most days. Still,
I know better. Grief.
Grief got hold of her like the left side of bad luck and
Never let go. Finally,
She has peace.

Hurricanes & Hallelujahs

Hurricane Days

These are days of heavy rains & hurricanes
Booming thunder, lightning & sultry nights
When bedsheets stick &
'Squitoes follow your skin
Hum a tease in your ear side up
Stinging & blood-sucking while you
Sleep if you can
Water bugs rise from sink drains, from
Deeper pipes, mice or rats visit toilets and
Private parts of unaware sitters in the dark
Between thunderclaps that
Echo wars of the past &
Inner wars of the present—
Absent love or hearts heavy with jealousy or
Love family full of face with empty pockets—
When the lights fail
All electrical sound stops
Not even white noise
No birds yak no dogs bark
We marvel at jagged light, 200
Streaks across grey-black skies
When the air cools &
Smells freshly washed in
Thundershowers like bombs of water falling
We give thanks for such
Reminders, what's important
Being here

We Leave Today

Today, a hurricane draws near
Radar draws a swirl too wide too close too bold
Like a fan over the mouth of the Gulf, its face
Hidden by the lace pattern of cloud and storms.
Folks told today, it's time to
Fear the winds, and the waves will
Wash this city away
Fold its buildings like bent cardboard
Don't stay they say, if
Alone, there'll be no one here to help
No phones will work
No water will be safe
Don't fret just
Pack a change of clothes
Return in three days when the
Hurricane inhabits another space, so
We leave to drive to
Sit and pray to Our Lady of Prompt Succor, our
Intercessor in such times of need, she's a
Miracle maker, a promise keeper,
Mother of our Savior, so we pray,
Drive, and sit on hold.

Hurricane Signs

When you see
I-10 signs beheaded
Their downtown arrow
Points to grey sky
Denying the logic of direction
Announcing its new calling
Lagniappe from hurricanes, tornadoes
Highway signs
Beaten to broken
Like half a giraffe.

Hurricane Lesson #6

Welcome to our world:
Hurricane 101, we prep for
Days or weeks of no lights,
Eat leftovers & fruit first, then
No fresh food, only canned &
Water stored, or
Pack what you can carry,
Evacuate to safety, and
Pray till it passes.
Big Bad Hurricane Irene
Huffed, puffed & didn't
Sink the South but drenched the
Northeast coast on the
6th anniversary of American Shame, the
Government & media response to Irene
Stronger than her wet slaps; still,
Gothamites missed their
Subways, eateries, lights
Great grouches, no greater abuse to
New York City than inconvenience.

2011 September 2nd, "Apocalypse Not" the
New York Post proclaims;
"One for the CYA age" (*WSJ* Bret Stephens),
Manhattan evacuates to
Prep for the worse, then
Folks wash out from
North Carolina to New Jersey to Vermont, they
Know: not slapping blame but

Saving lives matters,
Our nation, our people,
Need each other now.

New Orleans
Archdioceses Announces
Church Closings

Church, the place parents send kids on Sundays.
For some it's duty, weekly rhythm like work & weekends.
For us, it's God's house, where we honor His love,
Give thanks for grace, celebrate our ancestors,
Baptize our babies, confirm our teens, marry
Couples, and give rocking home-goings before
Burying our dead—the departed, preparation for the
Life after now, a better place, free of the pains and
Troubles of this life, so we cherish memories of lives
Well lived, and say goodbye, before we begin again. The
Next day, the next week.

Churches do not erupt like volcanoes,
They are built brick by brick, nickel by dollar,
Sacrifice by savings, bake sales by cookouts,
Dances for dimes, dollars for little scholars,
Potlucks by the faithful, who tithe their time,
Talents, and income believing the temple to come
Will nourish their families and souls into the sacred,
Teach the Good Book, the right ways, provide a comfort from
The world's weariness and a healing for sick hearts
Often dented by hurts that daily life piles on us.

These temples teach us that God is everywhere,
All the time, but in this place, God is surely with us,
And when we come here, we feel it; we hear it in
Standard gospel phrases into a Fred Hammond song:
    "This is the day the Lord has made

We should be glad about it.
Everybody rejoice! Come on everybody rejoice!
Sing praises to his holy name."
We sing, we chant, we moan, we give thanks, and
We are healed for now; we rise in sound of praise, and
We float home, from God's house, hopeful for tomorrow.

Southern Sky

Driving down I-10 East, Louisiana interstate
Squeezed between a black compact a
White semitruck with no trailer, the
Heat index 105, the AC
Humming a cool tune, today's
Bedroom-blue sky,
How many storms know this sky?
Bedroom-blue sky punctuated with
Dirty cotton clouds; oh no
Smoke, sandy bubbling rising
Whiter on the eastern horizon. The
Swamp's on fire
Stinks like rotting rats; this
Eastern route darkens by smoke not storms.

Fire theories rise like the stinky
Smoke across this blue horizon.
Heat lightning or an oil rig?
Corruption? Chaos, thinking stolen by smoke,
Just smoke, smoldering, hugging evergreen treetops
Charring *cinnamomum camphora*, toxic to native pine,
Chinaberry, peat moss, nutria fleeing fire & smoke
Pine fizzes, and smoke pours dark poufs in daylight.
Folks asthmatic choke, sinuses drain,
Faces sneeze, wheeze, snot
Not a dry eye in the Crescent City
Watery eyes blink swamp smoke
Folks clack complaints
Like ducks squawking by surprise,

Smoke-filled haze covers skies.
Aunt Rose says:
"Thank God for eyes to see."

Hurricane Gustav @ JJ's

—For Joyce Jackson

Beloved New Orleans
Emptying like a cereal bowl,
Residents flee for the second mandatory evacuation in history,
Spilling onto I-10
Highways, all roads out
Bumper to bumper,
Cars going anywhere but here
Where Gustav knocks with
Intermittent bursts of rain spraying into
Thunderous downfalls,
Humbling stately oaks, pine, people.

JJ's home a haven for the weary
Like me, Miz Litdell, Queen Mother of the
Creole Wild West, Black Indian Tribe, who
Mask at Mardi Gras, St. Joseph's—
Patron saint of working folks—Day, and
"Honey," Wild Man of the Creole Wild West.
Emptied from the Crescent City,
Together we fight lines for food, MREs,
Gas cues spiral like spider legs all for a
Gallon or two for generators and cars.
We give thanks for the quiet of no power
Save the hand-crank radio, and I
Listen to Creole Wild West recent glories
New suits fanned in purple plumes parading for the neighborhood.

I snatch these lines between JJ's amens on Mardi Gras Indian tales,
    between
Waves of Gustav's rain. There's
No similes in Gustav's eye, only the
Blue space of azure sky, then
Gunmetal grey clouds cover,
Brazen like a blind Black samurai on street corners.
Raindrops stop
Sunlight sneaks a smile, a
Ray of hope between
Wide coughing winds.

Hurricane Lessons
Isaac September & Sandy October

Disasters invite blame for local officials, government, ignoring
Geography. We meet geography in fourth-grade classes of
Elementary schools, and rarely revisit until college if
You're lucky. Then, you learn of morrains, and how the flow of
Ice leaves hills and valleys in their wake, how old the
Grand Canyon really is, and how any coastline is a
Hurricane or typhoon hit-list target.

Post-Katrina flooding was an unnatural disaster to a
Beautiful city below sea level, a city whose typography
Scoops are the neighborhoods making culture almost four
Centuries old and still warming the world with wonder.

We hunker down during Isaac, wake to thousands of dollars of
Wind damage and flooding. The week and a half without
Electricity a respite from the business of the fall term,
Deadlines we paint onto calendars, and many delays
Follow us as food spoils and thaws too quickly. We
Greet neighbors we rarely see these days of driving
Across town to shop, escaping "food deserts" and the loss of
Corner stores. I remember, two-plus years post-Katrina, we
Danced the Second Line when the first Walgreens returned. At
Least this time, we still have our homes, our books and music,
Our kitchens and "whatnots." Whole 100-year-old live oak trees
    demolish a
House down the block on Pauger Street; the cement and fiberglass
Backer boards and wrap on my home-in-progress blown forty ways to
Sunday, fan debris on sidewalks, the street. Cleanup is slow.

North shore of Lake Ponchartrain residents blame New Orleans' new
      levees. We all wait for
Insurance claims adjusters; weep at the 5 percent wind deductible, even
      for homes incomplete.

We watch in horror: Sandy's swirls along the Northeast coast,
Shudder to think of the fallout from the flooding to come. Like Isaac,
      Sandy is an
Equal Opportunity Disaster, hitting the top percent New Jersey shore-
      line residents as
Well as the New York City subway system. We host prayer vigils,
      pinch the
Pennies in our pockets to donate something, anything, to help; we
      know the
Long road ahead the Northeast faces, and we send what we can, while
Complaints rise with weather reports, hope for better understanding of
Geography and generosity.

Presidential Poems

God Bless President Obama
& the United States of America

We've been fighting
Fighting, fighting
For freedom
Since Virginia's first Black backs
Went from indentured servants
To slaves overnight
We've been fighting
Fighting, fighting
Almost 400 years
Almost 4 centuries
Fighting the specter of racism
Till November 4th 2008
When 100-year-old women and men
Black, Brown, Red, white, and Yellow, of every faith and creed
Native and newly naturalized citizens
Pressed buttons pushing votes
To change our lives forever
To turn hope into possibility
To say "no to welfare for Wall Street
Without help for Main Street"
To say yes to a future with the promise
To fulfill the American dream
To bring America back to democracy
To say no to a past of pain
To say no to indifference and yes to equality
To say no to fear and yes to faith in tomorrow
Thank you all. God bless America.

The Night America Elected the First Black President

All day, my students asked:
What were you doing last night Doc?
Last night? November 4, 2008?
When American history exploded
Transported more than half a nation
Into a frenzy, into shock, into smiles and more shock?
I cried, cried, cried again, big ballooka tears raining down
My face, clogging my nose; my eyes leaked until
Words escaped me, until joy covered me in a
Blanket of tears and rain, tears erasing doubt,
Tears writing hope across my cheeks, streaked,
Fear drowning in tears.
I cried for Emmett Till, for Malcolm X, for JFK, for my grandfather
Frank who was born a slave in Sumter, Alabama, and walked to
New Orleans to be free, but landed in Laurel, Mississippi; so for
Most of my life, I thought he'd left slavery along the Natchez Trace,
Stealing into swamps by day, saved by Natives—some Natchez, then
    Choctaw or Houma by night—hopping over alligators and slave catchers
Muddy mounds, and braving thundershowers under palmetto palms
I cried for Harriet Tubman leading escaping slaves in sorrow songs
    by day and the twinkle of the drinking gourd by moonlit nights;
    for Zora Neale Hurston traversing the Gulf Coast driving unlit
    unpaved roads from Florida to Louisiana to catch tales we love we
    need amid jim crow and ku klux klan country carving a career and
    preserving our culture;
I cried for Martin Luther King, for Robert Kennedy, for Fannie Lou
    Hamer & all the Fannie Lous so sick and tired of being sick and
    tired. I cried for my chocolate-faced mother who had to explain
    too many times whose pale-olive baby she was keeping when they

saw me in tow, hanging onto her skirts, and breath, stories, and
     wisdom.
Last night, I cried for all those shoulders, backs, and bridges Barack
     Hussein Obama climbed to become the 44th president of the
     United States of America.
I cried for joy because for the first time in my life,
America, all these smiling faces in Chicago's Grant Park, a rainbow in
     faces,
Crying joyful rain with me, rejoicing realize
America is its people, all of its people,
All of them, all of us,
We, as one nation under God.
God bless us all. Now, pinch me.

Lincoln in New Orleans, 1831

—for President Obama, February 12, 2009

Abraham Lincoln was raised
To farm feeding, hoeing, mending a
Life in "unbroken forest," a full fight with
Trees, logs, and grubs. Abe
Read, wrote, and ciphered to
The Rule of Three when the Lincolns
Moved to Indiana in 1816, partly
On account of slavery, his parents
Baptist, and "naturally anti-slavery," so
Abe never remembered when he
Did not think so and feel so.
1828, Abe lost his sister in childbirth, and
He shoved and rowed on his first
flatboat trip down the Mississippi to
New Orleans, muddy with merchants,
Mulatto mistresses, and brown-faced folks
Shackled like cows, with eyes seeking sanctuary.
By 1831, Abe floated again to the Crescent City
His second flatboat trip down the 'Sippi
Into Jackson Square, the St. Louis Cathedral
Standing in majesty, framing the river, like the
Auction block, where brown-eyed picaninnies cried
Being torn from mothers, dreaming of fathers for rescue, and
Abe Lincoln learning horror firsthand.

We

Not you, not me, not he, not she, just us
We the people. We the brave.
We the heart. We the folk.
Not Republican, not Democrat
Not Independent.
Not Christian, not Jew,
Not Muslim, not Catholic
Not Baha'i, not Buddhist
Not Mormon, not Methodist
Not Lutheran, not Anglican.
We, together for
Our greater good,
Not upper class
Not lower class, not middle class,
Not white, not Black,
Not Red, not Brown,
Not Yellow like the sun,
Only us, a
Force against ignorance, a
Coat of We
To comfort the afflicted.

We, wrapped in together
A brace for cold or war or wind
A shelter against poverty and pain,
We, bread for a nation of neighbors,
A foundation for our future,
Neighbors to the world,
To work against poverty
Defend the helpless
Promote justice

Advance liberty.
We the people
Must remember:

> "America! America!
> God shed his grace on thee,
> And crown thy good
> with brotherhood . . ."

America, it is to us this land
of Black and Brown and Red and white, Yellow
from sea to shining face to hug our faith
our parents made as firm as bold past strain
not prejudice not poor, but our future,
our folk to build a safe big world, and free
our land, the world, neighbors, all of us, forever.
We, all of us—
Actors to carpenters, cooks to caregivers, bakers to farmers,
     postal workers to fishermen, artists to engineers—
We the people
Are one nation
Here to honor
The good, the great
Our leaders who work
To wake us—
We, sometimes, drunk
From the muck
Of the world—
To make life better,
You, who show courage
In the face of cowardice
To save the world.

Liberty Medal recipients:
We honor your work.

"Lift every voice and sing
Till earth and heaven ring
Ring with the harmonies
Of liberty . . . "

We honor your work,
How you call us
How you urge us
Into one people
For our greater good.

President George H. W. Bush and
President William J. Clinton,
We honor your work.
We the people, honor your work:

for our nations:	Yes
for our peace:	*Na'm*
for our world:	*Shi*
for our hopes:	*Oui*
for our good:	*Ken*
for our future:	*Ha'i*
for our neighbors:	*Ja*
for one world:	*Neah*
for our posterity:	*Sí*
for our common good:	*Oh Oh.*

We give thanks.

Four More Years
for President Obama

Let the history of America say freedom of speech took a left
Turn down shrill and insult, then landed on Poor Taste Street.
Note Republican lies:
>"He's Kenyan not American!
>He doesn't have an American birth certificate!
>He's a Muslim radical undercover of politics."

Plus truth:
American Wichita, Kansas Mom; from Kenyan Dad who
Grew up herding goats, earned University of Hawaii scholarship,
Manoa educated to Harvard PhD. Now President Obama,
Born in Honolulu, Hawaii, USA graduated Harvard Law in 1988, met
Michelle Robinson, his advisor in a summer internship
Elected 1st African American editor, *Harvard Law Review,*
Magna cum laude graduate 1991; how American is that?

Add history-making presidency
2008, elected hope for humanity
Saved jobs, bailed out the auto industry
Gave us historic free health care, an American first.

Add 208 schemes:
>208 Republican bills to intimidate the poor
>208 attempts at voter suppression

Subtract international support:
Kenyans think he's Kenyan
Ghanaians, Malians, Senegalese, Zulu
Columbians, Panamanians, Italians,
French, German, British, Chinese,

Japanese agree he's a first-class American world citizen, the
Best hope of the democratic ideal for the world.
Americans confirm: four more years for President Obama.
We give thanks and look forward to a future for all of us.

Second Lines
New Orleans Matters

Stolen Moments

Southern, this space
Crescent the city
Cradled like a mother's arms or
Allah's sickle framing a heavenly star
We like it like that, cozy, the
Comfort of a familiar banquette
That's why we
Give people the time of day
Ask about ya mamma 'n'em—
A sidewalk rite of passage

Louisiana Lore

Why go barefoot in Louisiana?
Holy ground
American by birth
Louisianans by grace
God's country,
Chaque corps importe
(Everybody matters)
New Orleans, a
Creole country
By baptism, a
Local call to God

New Orleans
More Holy than You Think

Hey now Media, the
Next time you flash breasts flying bare on Bourbon Street
Fan New Orleans neighborhoods, aim for fresh
Close-ups of corner bars, then churches
Block-for-block, there're more churches than bars, churches
Tall ones, arched cathedral-like or
Carved, Spanish mission-like in adobe or brick, or short
Storefronts, still sporting glass windows that used to
Showcase dry goods, or daily hot sausage specials
Marquees announcing the Good Book's message of the day, then
Women & men, kids of all shades and faiths
Pouring into and out of study & worship.
It's a family thing, our neighborhoods,
Our homes adorned with altars year round
Grottos of honor to St. Francis of Assisi, patron
Saint of animals, gardens, the
Blessed Mother guarding sidewalks and lawns, or
St. Joseph, patron saint of husbands & fathers,
Working men & women, of departing souls,
St. Joseph, flanked with beans,
Beads, and candles lit in
Prayers of the faithful; this is the
New Orleans we know, solid as the
Rocks of ages

This 5th August since Katrina

There are
5 SUNDAYS,
5 MONDAYS
5 TUESDAYS this month.
This happens once in 823 years.
After summeritis, just
What we need: extra working days.

It's noon, and
Cicadas scream outside already,
Couldn't wait till later.
What do they know that we don't?
Oil coats brown pelicans,
Sea turtles, *cawain* we stew.
Instead of asking, "how's ya mamma 'n'em?" We ask
  "How's the oysters, shrimp?"
  "High as Louisiana Pines yeah!"
  "Sho' you right. So, what about gumbo this fall?"
  "How we gonna stuff meliton for Thanksgiving with no
  shrimp?"
  "Shrimp?"
  "Awww, the Good Lord made the shrimp!" "An'
If the Lord says the same, shrimp's gonna
Swim in my gumbo come cold breezes."
  "Sho' you right."
  "Yes indeed."
  "The Good Lord's
  Gonna keep shrimp & oysters floatin' from
  Now till kingdom come."

Sundays in New Orleans

We visit mysteries
We cannot see
Forgiveness yellow
Penance purple
Crucifixion red
Resurrection white
We learn that change is
God's gift
No two leaves; no two clouds
No two stars; no two skies
No two hands or hurricanes
No two faces; no two smiles
No two birds; no two rocks
No two days ever alike.
Sacred songs fill our chests,
Full of peace,
Overflowing with possibility.
Hope crowns the
Muddy Mississippi
Cradles the Crescent City
Punctuates the steps to nowhere, the
Spaces between neighbors'
Katrina-beaten doorways, families
Too stubborn to leave sidewalks that
Echo Creole generations of *la joie de vivre*. Our
City blocks, from the Ninth Ward to the
Seventh Ward to midcity, smile
Toothless, missing homes now demolished,
Families lost to Gonzales, Vacherie, Houston
Black-lanta and all points out of here.
Homes standing rebuilt, some new

High as young oak trees,
Bought with fortitude, heart, patience, more
Penance paid to faceless government loans, a few
Government grants spread willy-nilly avoiding need.
So, Sundays, we
Thank You Jesus
We made it over
We made it over.

Who hates hurricanes?

Who hates hurricanes?
Clap your hands!
Clap your hands!

Who loves to party?
Clap your hands!
Clap your hands!

What's the date? 12-01; 12-01
Holler: Bye-bye hurricanes, Bye-bye hurricanes
Clap your hands!
What's the date? 12-01; 12-01

Hurricane: pour 2 oz. light rum; 2 oz. dark rum; 2 oz. passion
    fruit juice
1 oz. orange juice or pineapple; squeeze half a lime;
Add 1 tsp. simple syrup + 1 tsp. grenadine
Add an orange slice with cherry for garnish,
If you hate hurricanes,
Try tequila & salt, or sugar from the cane
Touched only by rain, sucked straight from a stalk

Breezes waft of night jasmine
Camellia blooms blanket the banquet
Autumn nights humid like summer sweat
Sweet olive blossoms perfume evening strolls

Cel-e-brate, Cel-e-brate, the
End of storm season, we
Lift our eyes to the sky

Sunny smiling in a canopy of blue
Our Lady of Prompt Succor,
Protector of Gulf Peoples, thank you
November ends December comes, we
Celebrate, the
Reason for the season,
Peace comes in the morning,
We give thanks. Clap your hands!
We give thanks. Clap your hands!

100 Thousand Poets for Change

*—Café Istanbul, New Orleans, Louisiana,
29 September 2012*

Change! Not a noun for leftovers, but a verb, a
Shift in habit, change can
Alter color, mutate a lizard or
Convert a person, so
Change how you see folks
Add acceptance, tolerance
Subtract assumptions
Change how folks see you
Embrace honesty
Smile more
Change like you switch channels at TV commercials
Change like costs rise
Don L. Lee, a.k.a. Haki Madhubuti, taught
Niggas how to change their minds
Change like arithmetic matters, add ideas for yourself
Change yourself
Change your block
Change your community
Change your city
Change the world

Michael Rothenberg hiking in the redwood forests in
2011 struck by the power of words to
Unite artists & communities worldwide &
100 Thousand Poets for Change born, more than
600 poetry events in 95 countries, billed as the
Largest poetry event in history
Change yourself

Change your block
Change your community
Change your city
Change the world

Demonstrate together, from Mumbai to celebrating
Local Adivasi tribes in verse & song
Terelj, Mongolia honor poet R. Choinom—
Victim of the old socialist regime,
Africans in Brazzaville, Republic of the Congo change. Hey!
Hold a poetry slam, even
War-torn Kabul & Jalalabad, Afghanistan all Poets for Change did it!
    From
Santa Rosa, California, to New Orleans, Louisiana, urged by the call
    from
Chuck Perkins at Café Istanbul on North Rampart Street
Change yourself
Change your block
Change your community
Change your city
Change the world

From Barranquilla, Colombia to Patras, Greece, 2011 to
800 events in 115 countries, more than 550 cities
Poets & musicians for change 2012
Sing a happy song & change a mind
Joy is contagious
Peace is the best medicine
Protect humanity
Change yourself
Change your block
Change your community
Change your city
Change the world

Change politics to professions of
Truth; teach right from wrong, change
Shades of deceit to
Human rights for all
Stop accusing Americans for
Social Security payouts &
Medicaid coverage
Inform yourself
We paid for it all our working lives
Change yourself
Change your block
Change your community
Change your city
Change the world

Change Congress from
Democrat & Republican parties to
Americans for American people
Change campaign ads from
Attacking candidates to
Presenting truth bare for
Picking the best person for the job for the
American people, a leader for everyone not
One percent, but 100 percent of all the people
Change yourself
Change your block
Change your community
Change your city
Change the world

Change like our future depends on it
Change to make our air clean
Change to protect the earth
There are no do-overs, no refunds for this planet
Change anger to possibilities of difference

Change violent disputes to debates with respect
Change cursing to crusading for just causes
Change yourself
Change your block
Change your community
Change your city
Change the world

Change schools to add art for uplift, change to add
Physical education and music for greater health and whole human
    beings
Pass the bill to help everyone afford a college education
Keep pressing for better health care and options for prevention of
    diseases
Promote, support artists; everyone else in the world does—the
Arts write, draw, and sculpt our times better than the daily news
Change yourself
Change your block
Change your community
Change your city
Change the world

Change attacks & lies about President Obama from
Catholic bishops to bullying bigots & their
Chants of undivided loyalty; this is
America, land of the little guy, home of the hardworking
Return respect to our BIG Chief of the best country in the free world
Honor our president's accomplishments;
Express thanks for his service, his family, and good works
Change from contempt and racist remarks to
Embrace an America for every race, gender, and religion
Wear the shoe that fits you best, but
Don't deny my choices, my faith, my gender
Be a patriot; hire or house a veteran
Learn world history & geography

We're all talking geography since NYC & NJ flooded
Treasure ancestry
Learn from the past or repeat its pain

Change yourself
Change your block
Change your community
Change your city
Change the world

Stand when our National Anthem is sung
Place your hand over your heart and
Sing your heart out, for our country for
All those who died to protect our freedoms
Praise our leaders in service
Tell them when they help us
Tell them & fire them when they don't
Don't complain when you don't even vote
Hate the choices? Create better ones
Be the change you want
Go green & plant a tree
Save rainwater
Pick up trash
Report or stop a crime (anonymously of course)
Help an elder
Tutor a kid
Replace hate with love
Love yourself
Change yourself
Change your block
Change your community
Change your city
Change the world

From Lament to Hope

Since Katrina winds spread
Hundreds of miles wide across
Gulf of Mexico waters, when I,
All my family, extended family, and friends lost everything
I've lived on two coasts, 1 south, 1 Northwest, in
Two states, Louisiana & Washington, and
Piece-the-way in California
15 moves, 12 addresses, not uncommon,
Most folks moved 5 times before leaving Louisiana—
6 houses (one planned then aborted upon arrival)
3 apartment buildings
1 gutted shotgun
Now, a demolished 105-year-old
Treasure bought for $2,000 on the
GI Bill post–WWII by my
Creole Sergeant Daddy. Since then,
4 sets of architectural plans:
1st set to raise the 2200 sq. ft. shotgun over
Water lines staining my heart & head still; the
$100,000 cost to elevate it and termite-eaten wood
Nixed keeping our family place;
Just not worth it; no one mills wood that thick anymore.
3 more sets of house plans:
1 geotech survey, a
Pile-load text
To reduce 120 pilings to
45, saving thousands of bucks.

I returned from Seattle
Summer 2007, was
Hit by a car walking behind NOMA, in

City Park, City Park
2nd in size to Central Park in NYC
Hit & run, a brotha, 7:30 a.m., before church
Didn't break a bone
Thank God! It
Took months to
Locate pain's source, then
Shoulder surgery
Summer 2008, two
Years of hurt and healing
Now finally back to me
In time for
Two hearings before the City Council
One for demolition
One for zoning by history not
Gentrification standards

My eyes only leak
When reunited with family or at funerals for
Faithful Creoles broken by disappointment &
Stress of living stranded, beaten by turnstile rulings
Neighbors still exiled because of
Health or lack of access to funding or just
Too beat up to risk such
Devastation, disappointment again

I give thanks
I was never in a shelter
Always welcomed by dear friends & family able
To offer hospitality.
I'm replacing my 105-year-old stick-built childhood home with
Concrete and steel. I
Return to my Creole neighborhood
My Black Creole Catholic church
Family—St. Raymond

Now combined with St. Leo the Great,
Where during jim crow
Colored kids couldn't walk their sidewalk even in rain;
If let in, we had to sit in the last two pews
Now allowed to take communion.
From what was to what St. Leo is now—coupled with St. Raymond
Black with a Black pastor &
Some white members, loving the
Holy & rocking mix. I'm home again.
Look what the Lord has done.

Blessed Be Us

Blessed are the mothers and fathers
Who daughter and son, and
Cousin, aunt, or
Parrain, and uncle, to friends and neighbors.

Blessed be the Maw Maws, Ma Dears,
Paw Paws, or Big Maws,
Big Pappas & Big Mammas who begot the
Mothers and fathers and
Loved them all.

Blessed is the love of daughter and son, who live the love, and pass it on.
Blessed be the 20 kids and 6 others murdered at Sandy Hook school
Blessed be their families, friends, loved ones, neighbors, their town
    folk, in Connecticut
Blessed be Newtown's grief, loss, and shock, and the grief, loss, and
    shock
We all feel for you, as a nation, as human beings, Americans about to
Celebrate the holy Christmastime; we cry with you; we hurt with you.
Blessed be the kids killed by kids for play, their loss, their lives and loves
Blessed be the kids killed by crossfire, murdered, snuffed from life and
    love in
All the cities of our nation, kids erased from a future, heaven sent too
    soon.
Blessed be all those shot in the 2013 Mother's Day Massacre,
During a Seventh Ward Second Line, a sacred tradition, revelers
Parading for our culture, neighborhoods, for ourselves, visitors, press.

Blessed be the friend and neighbor, who love the mothers and fathers
    and

Daughters and sons, cousins, aunts, *parrains*, and uncles, who raise the love
    the love
Root it deep, water with compassion, support its branches like the
Walls of a house
Roofed in wishes of joy that
Smoke happiness.

Blessed be the Maker, *Pappa Nou*! Our Father, Our God!
Who gives us the love.

New Orleans,
a Neighborhood Nation

Possums sleep, middle of the road sometimes,
Invade soggy walls after hurricanes dump heavy rains,
Hide in clothes closets and eat through my canvas book bags
Must taste like peanut butter and strawberry jam, the
Pages of wisdom spread like confetti on the floor.

10,000 spiders live in my neighborhood.
What grows wild sticks like thorns
What crawls will bite you red and blue
Roaches spread wings past dusk, invade doorjambs
We grow, eat, and love okra; there
Ain't no proper gravy without a little slime
Veggie slimes are us Black folks on this planet

We know folks backwards and forwards
Translate: to every little thing, nothing forgotten

Y'all is singular, plural, and a sweet sound in our ears
Festivals are us: shrimp, satsumas, tomato, rice, crawfish, blues & jazz

We throw hissy fits in a heartbeat
Find cayenne, salt, onion, celery, parsley, and thyme on
Yard birds baked, fried, or stewed, even on the other
White meat, anything that swims in a bayou, lake or river:
Catfish, grouper, red fish, crab, sheephead, *cawain.*
Out of bread? Whip up *gallait* or fritters deep-fried with
Ripe bananas or a pocket of plantains in season; just honey to taste.

When weather dips below 70, not too low our
Winters without cold, then it's gumbo time.
Okra, seafood, or beans *de jour*: red beans, white beans, butter beans,
    crowder peas
Plus black-eyed peas, the eyes of God on us

We still make hucklebucks in summer
Make suppers to raise bucks for folks stuck between a
Rock & a hard place, and pass potato salad over a
Fence for a backyard barbeque with hot beer and
Hurricane cocktails at sunset in yards or on
Galleries glad for time measured in minutes.

New Orleans Matters

Crescent City, New Orleans so
Named for a bend in the river, is a
Lot more than the
Cradle of jazz.

Hook, line & sinker
New Orleans is cradle to rhythm & blues
From Huey Smith's "I've Got the
Rockin' Pneumonia and the
Boogie Woogie Flu!"
      "I wanna jump but I'm afraid I'll fall
      I wanna holler but the joint's too small
      Young man rhythm's got a hold of me too
      I've got the rockin' pneumonia and the boogie woogie flu."

Resonating R & B like
Ray Charles' "I've Got a Woman"
      "Way over town
        That's good to me (eee)
        Ohhh yeah!"
Recorded here circa 1955
Soothing R & B like
Allen Toussaint's
"Ruler of My Heart"
      "Ruler of my heart
      America, driver of U.S. souls,
      Help me please.
      Where can you be?"
Or the
"Lipstick traces" of neighborhood footprints
Abandoned like

Old lovers whose future is
Foretold in
Black lives lined like spoons on slave ships or
After Katrina, Blacks
Lined along Superdome stairs on the
6 o'clock blues
New Orleans, cradle of
Rock and roll, like
Lady Marmalade:
       "Voulez-vouz couchez avec moi ce soir?"
Not New Orleans,
Stagnant like Katrina waters until the
Meters sing "They All Ask'd For You"
       "I went on down to the Audubon Zoo
       And they all asked for you.
       The monkey asked
       The tiger asked
       And the elephant asked me too."

From Seattle to NYC, like Fats
Domino's singing, just bent a little here
       We lost our thrill, on
       "Blueberry Hill.
       We linger until"
Blues wakes us and woos us to sleep,
Then we begin
       "Walking to New Orleans" (1960)
Any way we can.

Those of us home again feel like
Lee Dorsey's 1966 hit
       "Working In The Coal Mine"
       Lookin' for our hometown
       Workin' in the U.S. town
       Woops, feeling let down

Just add Alan Toussaint's "Mother-in-Law" (1961)
Plus his Pointer Sisters '70s hit:
      "I know we can make it
      I know that we can
      I know we can work it out!
      Yes we can, can
      Yes we can, can"

New Orleans cradle of blues, funk, jazz
Rhythm & blues, and a
Whole lot of other
Beats the world can't seem to live without.
"We like it like that" Toussaint says;
Everything we do's gonna be funky!

Eight years post-Katrina (though
We beat poor predictions of our demise),
We hold what happy we can
New Orleans needs help still
Abandoned homes & steps to nowhere
Left to rot like the blighted homes,
Leaning, barely standing.

We ain't dying y'all; like roaches
We can't be buried.
We rise after funerals!
Ever heard of a Second Line?
We live, celebrate lives in beats, songs, and dances.

So what can blues, jazz, R & B fans do?
Come & visit September to May when
Southern skies smile on us; or,
Brave brutal heat, June to early fall;
Help us with harangues to Congress; help
New Orleans,

Mother-ship to music,
Begin a Crescent City Crusade, a
Healing for our hearts and home.

Notes

"Missing in 2005: Neighborhood Necessities": Before NOLA response, before the federal government, before churches or any faith-based rescue organizations, before charities, the first institutions to help were neighborhood bars, in particular Bullet's Bar; it was the only light visible downtown from the air or interstate. Bullet's Bar had ice, food, lights, an oasis in the aftermath of the unnatural post-Katrina flooding disaster.

"Iraq by the Numbers": 21 October 2011, President Barack Obama announced Iraq accepts responsibility for its own safety, and American troops went home for Christmas.

"My Race": white supremacy and anti-Black prejudice and racism from whites and Blacks.

"2 Friends": DeBose Fine Arts Festival is an annual event in Baton Rouge; Cindy Lou Levee helped organize the event post-Katrina.

"She was not a queen": The original photo is dated October 15, 1943. On the back side, my brother John wrote as dictated by his high school teacher this promise: "I am going to lead a life of a man of integrity, intelligence, and of noble deeds for the rest of my life." Signed by John Jr., 20 February 1947. A career Air Force and family man, he achieved all that and more.

"Creole Daddy Ways": My maternal grandfather cofounded Mount Zion Baptist Church on North Robinson, though he belonged first to the Rising Sun Baptist Church, which changed its name because of World War II and Japan to Rock of Ages. (John Jr. also says our mother was Catholic when she was first married to his papa and was christened at St. Rose of Lima on Bayou Road. Perhaps the pressure of being a preacher's kid brought her back to the Baptist church. In those days such divisions in practicing faiths were massive.)

"Lincoln in New Orleans": Composed for the occasion of the Lincoln Bicentennial 2009 held at Dillard University in concert with a request from then Louisiana Poet Laureate Darrell Bourque.

"We": A poem in celebration of President George H. W. Bush and President William Jefferson Clinton, 2006 Liberty Medal recipients, for the ceremony at the National Constitution Center in Philadelphia.

"We": From the song "America the Beautiful"; words by Katharine Lee Bates, melody by Samuel Ward.

"We": From the song "Lift Ev'ry Voice and Sing," also known as "The Black National Anthem"; words by James Weldon Johnson, melody by J. Rosamond Johnson.

"We": *Yes*, in English, Arabic, Chinese, French, Hebrew, Japanese, German and Swedish, Korean, Spanish and Italian, and Tagalog. Tagalog is one of the major languages of the Philippines, has a close affinity with Malay languages (Bahasa Indonesia/Malay), and is the second most commonly spoken Asian language (after Chinese) in the United States, according to the 2000 Census. It is also the sixth most commonly spoken non-English language in America.

"This 5th August since Katrina": *Meliton* is colloquial for *mirliton*, a principal food of the Aztecs, Creoles, and Mayas, grows wild and is cultivated; also known as chayote, mango squash, or vegetable pear. It can be fried, stuffed, pickled, stir fried, cooked with tomatoes, and used in salad; stuffed is the favorite form in Louisiana.

Glossary

bébé: Creole and French for *baby*, a term of endearment used to address any age.

cicadas: "The loudest insect in our area is the cicada. It is often erroneously called a locust, but it doesn't hop about as do the grasshoppers and crickets, preferring instead to fly quickly, land, then sit still. Cajuns call them *cigale de bois*, meaning mosquito hawk of the woods, or *cigale de nuit*—mosquito hawk of the night" (Bob Thomas, *Nature Notes*, "Cicadas," September 9, 2009, http://loyno.edu/lucec/natural-history-writings/cicadas-0).

coon can: a street game for guys, a kind of street hockey where guys kick a can or hit it with a stick.

Étoufée Talk: Sweet talk, *étoufée*, a stew of usually crawfish, which is seasonal only and therefore special, then adding "talk" to make "special talk" or "sweet talk."

"food deserts": Massive areas without grocery stores or any healthful food businesses, largely in low-income areas. "While New Orleans had thirty-eight full-service grocery stores in August 2005, it only has eighteen today, even though 70 percent of the city's population has returned since Hurricane Katrina. Most of the grocery stores that have reopened are in wealthier neighborhoods: a 2007 Tulane University study found that 60 percent of low-income residents of New Orleans must drive more than three miles to go to a grocery store, and only half of those surveyed have a car" (Rebecca Mowgray, *The Times Picayune*, Sunday, October 9, 2011).

grand(e) mati: Familiar form of the Creole for "big lie" and colloquial for the f. *grande menti*, from the French *mentir*, "to tell a lie."

hallelujah: Hebrew for "praise God."

Holy Family nun: Sisters of the Holy Family, a Catholic religious order of Black nuns cofounded in New Orleans in 1842 by the Honorable Henriette Delille, a free woman of color. When children were left homeless by the pestilence in 1853, the sisters cared for the orphans. In 1892, the St. John Berchmans' Orphanage was dedicated. During the 1897 yellow fever epidemic in New Orleans, the Sisters of the Holy Family cared for the sick.

homebwoi: popularized by the Ying Yang Twins, colloquial for home-boy.

hucklebucks: frozen drinks or frozen juice in cups, sometimes called "zips" or "Dixie cups."

Papa nou or *Papa Nous:* Creole for "Our Father" or "Our God."

pas connais: Creole and Old French for "I don't know."

R month: Long thought an old wives tale, refers to months that end in an R, meaning cooler (Gulf-water) months, when oysters are natu-rally safer to eat; this was especially significant prior to the farming of oysters.

Sankofa: Akan, a West African culture, language, and symbol, for "looking back to go forward"; in other words, we learn of and reclaim our past to learn who we are, how we came to be today, which allows us to move ahead from strength of knowledge and a foundation built on the past.

Second Lines: They are NOT the line behind musicians. The second line, as celebrated in New Orleans has its roots in West Africa, where folks still parade with parasols (umbrellas) and dance with handker-chiefs. In New Orleans, the Second Line is a practice that dates to before the city was founded. The First Line is the procession to the graveyard, accompanied by a dirge; the Second Line is the return from the burial and is a celebration of the life lived, a celebration that all of your loved one's worries of this life are over and they are in a bet-ter place. Such celebrating of the previous, earthly life completes the mourning, allowing folks to move on and begin new days of living. This was particularly significant during slavery and jim crow, there-fore Second Lines are charged with a spirit of joy. This joyful post-burial celebration that has struck a strong chord with visitors and is still a significant and much-beloved part of our NOLA culture.

Social Aid and Pleasure Clubs: In New Orleans, many Black men join "societies," clubs that party with a purpose. These organizations grew out of the tradition of secret male societies common in West Africa from Mali to Ghana, where men joined together in groups for educational efforts, political survival, and social necessities. That tradition combined with Congo Square Sunday dancing and evolved into what we call today "benevolent societies," which foster similar moral interests and assist members with expenses for things such as funerals and education. Also, these societies provide an important social outlet during segregated times and enable individuals to survive in style and grace. For more information, see John W. Blassingame, *Black New Orleans: 1860–1880*; and Maria Leach, *Funk & Wagnalls Standard Dictionary of Folklore Mythology and Legend*, 2:1031.

strawberry: crackhead whore who will cheat, lie, and steal to get crack.

tchopitoulas: Choctaw for "by the river" or "people who live by the river."

yard birds: lots of folks used to keep chickens in their yards for eggs and meat, so we call chickens "yard birds."

About the Author

Dr. Mona Lisa Saloy, author and folklorist, is currently professor of English at Dillard University. Her poems and scholarly articles have been published in *The Southern Poetry Anthology*, *Louisiana Folklore Miscellany*, *Children's Folklore Review*, *The Journal of Southern Linguistics*, and *PanAfrican Literary Journal*. She wrote the forward to *Night Sessions: Poems*, by David S. Cho (CavanKerry Press, 2011). Some of her articles on "toasts" and the lore of Black children are available online at the *Folklife in Louisiana* Web site (http://www.louisianafolklife. org/LT/creole_articles.html). Her completed screenplay, "Rocking for a Risen Savor," is in production negotiations. Dr. Saloy's first poetry book, *Red Beans and Ricely Yours* (Truman State University Press, 2006), won the 2005 T. S. Eliot Prize for Poetry and the 2006 PEN/ Oakland Josephine Miles Prize, and was a finalist for the Morgan Poetry Prize from Story-Line Press.

In October 2006, the National Constitution Center in Philadelphia commissioned Mona Lisa Saloy to compose and perform a poem celebrating the 2006 Liberty Medal recipients, President William J. Clinton and President George H. W. Bush. That poem, entitled "We," is included in this collection. Saloy received a New Orleans Jazz and Heritage Foundation Community Partnership Grant for archiving and a UNCF/Mellon Faculty Fellowship in fall 2012, the only full-semester leave granted nationally, which she used to complete this, her second collection of verse. On sabbatical leave through summer 2013 by a generous grant from the Andrew Mellon Foundation and with permission from Dillard University, Saloy advanced work on her manuscript, a collection on the folklore on play and a collection of essays on Black Creoles of New Orleans. She writes for those who don't or can't tell Creole cultural stories.

About the Artist

Richard C. Thomas, a native son of New Orleans, holds a bachelor of arts degree from Xavier University. An established artist, Thomas is noted for beautiful paintings and murals throughout the city, including a famed Mardi Gras poster, a New Orleans Jazz & Heritage Festival Poster, images of Louis Armstrong, Fats Domino, Mahalia Jackson, Lionel Hampton, and Pete Fountain, and murals lacing the Louis Armstrong International Airport in New Orleans and other public places. In 2013, Thomas was commissioned by KABOOM to direct thirty-five youth for the mural on play at historic Hunter's Field in New Orleans' Seventh Ward. He is a curator and leader who encourages the recognition of African American artists, a business owner of Pieces of Power youth group of Visual Jazz, Inc., and a consultant to museums and galleries in and outside of New Orleans. Thomas was an original advisor to YA/YA (Young Artists, Young Aspirations), a teacher for Talented in the Arts Program, an artist-in-residence for the New Orleans Center for the Creative Arts (NOCCA). Thomas was commissioned by the Public Art Committee of Waterloo, Iowa, for *We the People*, a mural eighteen months in the making, representing the many people and cultures journeying to Waterloo in search of hope and opportunity. A dad and consummate professional, Richard C. Thomas is one rare fine artist who excels at art education and is passionate about grooming young artists, some of whom he actively mentors. Thomas's passion is to get kids off the streets by using his talents and showing them theirs through his many workshops and seminars. As a motivational speaker, he earned awards for his contribution to the arts and building up people to create a better world around them. Richard C. Thomas is also a singer and jazz musician. Richard.c.thomas.5@facebook.com.